Sefer Ha-Aggadah

· · · · · · ·

The Book of Legends
for Young Readers

ક૭

Adapted from *The Book of Legends:*

Sefer Ha-Aggadah, translated by William G. Braude

from the classic Hebrew work *Sefer Ha-Aggadah*,

edited by Hayim Nahman Bialik and

Yehoshua Hana Ravnitzky.

SEYMOUR ROSSEL

Sefer Ha-Aggadah

· · · · · ·

The Book of Legends
for Young Readers

Illustrated by JUDY DICK

UAHC Press · New York

Library of Congress Cataloging-in-Publication Data

Rossel, Seymour.

Sefer ha-aggadah : the book of legends for young readers /
 adapted from Sefer ha-aggadah by Hayim Nahman Bialik
and Yehoshua Hana Ravnitzky [by] Seymour Rossel ;
illustrated by Judy Dick.

       p.   cm.

Includes bibliographical references.

ISBN 0-8074-0603-1 (alk. paper)

1. Bible stories, English—O.T. 2. Legends, Jewish.

I. Dick, Judy, ill. II. Sefer ha-aggadah. III. Title.

BM107.R67 1996   96-8558

296.1'9—dc20   CIP

                                  AC

This book is published by arrangement with Schocken Books, Inc.

This book is printed on acid-free paper

Manufactured in the United States of America

10 9 8 7 6 5 4 3 2 1

For Rikki—

May you never lack for

wondrous tales to tell.

S. R.

Contents

Introduction

The six parts of the classic *Sefer Ha-Aggadah*, "The Book of Legends," were first published in Hebrew in Odessa, Russia, between 1908 and 1911. By that time, Hayim Nahman Bialik was already famous as "the Hebrew national poet," and his friend and partner Yehoshua Hana Ravnitzky was well known as an editor, journalist, and publisher. Both were concerned about bringing ancient Hebrew to life as a modern language. They decided to collect the legends and stories of the sages of talmudic times and present them in Hebrew.

Aggadah means "legend," but Bialik and Ravnitzky knew that the word meant much more to the sages. Weaving stories around the Jewish heritage, the sages created a world filled with lessons and masterful teachings. These tales were shared at night by families in their homes. For the Jewish people through the ages, these stories were the magazines, books, radio, television, movies, and Internet. Stories were told and retold, traded, shaped, and embellished. Teachings were repeated in the name of the rabbis who had first taught them, and when the names of the rabbis had been forgotten, people just began the teachings with "Our sages taught..." or "Our rabbis said...." When people heard these words, they reacted the way we do today when someone begins, "Once upon a time ...."

The original *Sefer Ha-Aggadah* contains hundreds of stories, each one a gem, arranged into six parts. The first part is made up of legends about the Bible and its main characters and events. The second part contains stories of the sages themselves. The third part speaks of the people of Israel and their place in the world. The fourth part deals with legends about God and teachings about good and evil. The fifth part is a collection of legends about life in the Jewish community. And whatever would not fit into one of the other categories is found in part six—sayings; proverbs; teachings about nature; and even superstitions, witchcraft, and magical cures.

The first English-language translation of the entire *Sefer Ha-Aggadah* was completed by Rabbi William G. Braude in 1988 and published by Schocken Books in 1992. In 1993, the UAHC Press decided to create a version of this classic for young people. This first volume is the initial result of that undertaking.

Not all the legends told in the *Sefer Ha-Aggadah* are appropriate for young readers. Some contain complex concepts requiring detailed explanations that would detract from the liveliness of the tales. Even the legends selected for this collection had to be "unpacked" from their compact form. Wherever possible, the author retained the narrative as it was found in the original. From time to time, however, tales were combined and parts were rearranged to achieve for young readers the clarity and colorful narration of Bialik and Ravnitzky's original. Recapturing the excitement of our ancestors when they heard and told these stories, this volume will bring us closer to the precious heritage passed on in writing and by word of mouth from generation to generation.

Welcome to the world of Jewish legend and lore. Welcome to a world created in ancient times, arranged in modern times, and set before you as a gateway between the past and the future. May these tales bring you closer to God and God's creation and set your steps firmly on the pathways of peace.

§ 1 §

Light and Fire

God created Adam and taught him to speak, giving him words for all things around him: earth, wind, trees, flowers, fruits, and vines. God told Adam, "I created you today, on the sixth day of My creation."

Then God brought all the animals to Adam, two by two—one male and one female—and asked, "What will you name these animals?" And Adam gave names to the lions and the lambs, to the wolves and the kittens, to the crocodiles and the monkeys. He named the bees and the storks, the elks and the mountain goats. Adam was the first to call the worms "worms." He was the first to call the deer "deer."

Next God brought Adam to the middle of Eden's garden of trees and said, "You can eat of the fruit of every tree except this one. This is the tree of knowing good from evil. You may not eat its fruit. For now you know only good and live in peace and happiness. But if you eat the fruit of this tree, you will also know evil. And to know all things, you must also know death."

As the day wore on, God saw that Adam was growing sad. All the animals had mates. The lion had the lioness. The ram had the ewe. But Adam had no one. Then God said, "It is not right that Adam should be alone. I will make a mate just for him."

In this way, God became the first surgeon: God caused Adam to fall into a deep sleep. And while Adam was sleeping, God took one of Adam's ribs and used that rib to create a woman. When Adam awoke, he felt no pain, for at that time he knew only good and could not feel the evil of pain. He saw the woman standing alone, and he knew that she was meant for him. He said, "I will call her woman, for she came from man. She is the bone of my bone and the flesh of my flesh." And he was happy again, for now he had a mate. And she said, "My name is Eve."

It was still the sixth day when Adam and Eve together made the world's first mistake. Eve met the snake, and the snake said, "Go ahead, eat the fruit of the forbidden tree. It will not hurt you." Believing the snake, Eve ate the fruit and then shared it with Adam. "Now we shall be wise like God," they said to each other.

But Adam and Eve were no wiser. Instead, everything that had seemed good now seemed evil. Now they were afraid of the panthers and afraid of the crows. They were afraid of even the insects that crawled on the leaves and flew through the air.

When Adam and Eve heard the sound of God like a breeze passing through the garden, they were so frightened they ran to hide. And when God learned that they had eaten of the forbidden tree, God cursed the snake. God said to Adam and Eve, "Now that you know evil, you will also know pain. In the end, you will die and return to the earth." Then God took the man and the woman and sent them out of the Garden of Eden forever. "You have eaten enough from the trees of this garden," God said. "You must go out and rule over the earth. Follow My ways: Be fruitful and multiply."

As the sixth day ended, a strange thing happened: The sun dropped lower and lower in the western sky. Slowly, slowly the light of day began to fade away. Slowly, slowly the air grew colder. Adam and Eve were frightened to see the light dying. They huddled close together, warming each other. Even so, they soon began to shiver. And shivering frightened them even more.

All at once, the sun disappeared, and the world was darker than the inside of the darkest cave. "This must be our end," Adam worried. "Soon we will sink into the earth like the sun." And they were so tired and so afraid that they began to cry. "This must be the death of which God spoke," said Eve, weeping.

Magically, little fires lit the darkness. The first fire appeared just above their heads, then another one glowed far away in the distance. And so it went until the largest one of all began to rise. "It is like a little sun," said Eve. "Let's call it 'moon.'" And they named the tiny fires "stars."

All night long they huddled close, watching. "This cannot be death," said Eve. "See how the moon and the stars make the leaves glitter, and their light shines off the rabbits as they feed." "And see how the yellow eyes of the owls glow in the night," said Adam.

In this way the night passed. The light of dawn glowed red in the eastern sky until the sun rose to shed its golden rays. And God said, "This is My Sabbath. On this day, all shall rest." And Adam and Eve saw that it was good. "Night and day are the way of nature," they said. And they rested by the light of the day.

When the Sabbath day passed, the sun began to fall again in the sky. God said, "You shall not go into this new week in cold and fear. Behold, I am giving you a great gift. It is the gift of fire itself. If you are careful, you can control it. It will warm you by night and help you work by day."

Adam and Eve saw that it was good, and they praised God for the fire. So every week begins with blessing the fire of the *Havdalah* candle. And every week ends with blessing the fire of the Sabbath candles. [1,II:98 and 99]

From the Aggadah
NOAH AND THE LIE

Rabbi Levi taught: God decided to bring a flood to destroy all the evil in the world. Then how did the Lie survive?

All the creatures came to Noah's ark in pairs. While they were being loaded, the Lie tried to sneak into the ark, but Noah said, "You can't come aboard alone. God commanded that only partners could be saved." So the Lie found Beauty and said, "Be my mate." But Beauty took one look at the Lie and said, "You are too ugly for words." The Lie saw Truth and said, "Be my mate." But Truth said, "The two of us can never live together." Then the Lie saw Wickedness standing in a crowd of evil people, worshiping an idol. And the Lie said, "You are bad to look at and worse to smell. We were made for each other. Be my mate, and both of us can enter the ark and be saved from the flood."

Wickedness asked, "What will you give me?" The Lie thought and then answered, "I'll give you whatever can be gained by lying." Wickedness grinned a crooked grin and said, "That's all I'll ever need." So the two came to Noah, and he was forced to let them both enter the ark. And that is how the Lie survived, which is why people say, "Wickedness grows whenever the Lie is told." [1,II:132]

THE TOWER OF BABEL

The people said, "Let us build a tower to heaven so we can make war on God." And they began to build the tower. As the tower rose, the people had to carry the bricks to the top, one by one. The higher the tower, the longer it took to get a brick to the top. When the tower reached seven stories, it took a full day to carry one brick to the top.

When a person fell from the top, no one paid any attention. But when a brick fell from the top, all the workers sat down and wept. "It takes a very long time to get the bricks to the top," the people said to one another. Finally, God became angry and said, "They care more about the bricks than they do about one another. Then let them be like bricks speaking to one another." And God changed their one language into all the languages of the world. Now the people were truly like bricks, each one not understanding anything the others had to say. Thus, the place was called Babel because the people could only babble to one another. [1,II:138]

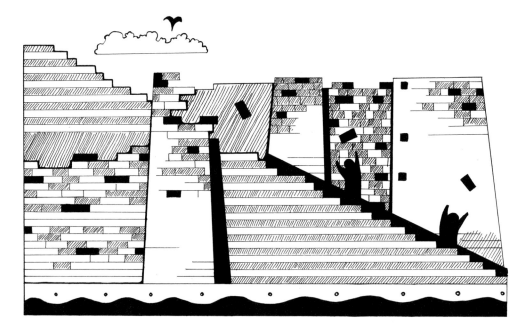

❦ 2 ❧

How Shall You Be Blessed?

Abraham and Sarah were growing old. Together, they had served God for many years, and God was very pleased with them. God spoke to the angels: "From the time of Adam to the time of Noah, I waited ten generations for a truly good person to appear in the world. Then, from the time of Noah to the time of Abraham and Sarah, I waited ten more generations for truly good people to appear."

"Now," said God, "I must show Abraham and Sarah how much I care for people who are good and walk in My ways. I must find a way to bless them."

One of the angels said, "What You ask, O God, is very difficult. How shall You bless them? Shall You bless them by making them upright and honest? They are already upright and honest."

Another angel said, "What You ask, O God, is very difficult. Shall You bless Abraham and Sarah by giving them love for each other? They already love each other."

And another angel said, "What You ask, O God, is very difficult. Shall You bless them by giving them wisdom? They are already wise."

At last, one of the older angels spoke: "Perhaps the answer may be found in a story."

God said, "Then tell your tale." And this is the story the angel told:

§ A man went wandering through the desert. He traveled for many days without finding a village or a town. He traveled for many days without finding a tree. He traveled for many days without finding water. He did not see animals along his way. And even the birds did not fly where he went.

Twenty days passed, and at the end of them he finally saw a tree standing alone in the distance. "I must go closer to this tree," he thought. "There may be water underneath it." And when he came up to the tree, he grew happy, for he saw that it stood over a little pool of water. He was very pleased, for the tree was green and full of dates, and beneath the tree was shade and a place to rest.

The man sat down beneath the tree, looking at its reflection on the water. When he was cooled by the shade, he picked some dates from the tree and ate them. Then he drank the water, and he felt refreshed. When he rose up to leave, he spoke to the tree.

"Tree, O tree," he said, "you have blessed me, and I would like to leave you with a blessing. But what blessing can I offer to you? Can I pray that your shade be pleasant? It is already pleasant. Can I pray that you grow straight and tall? You are already straight and tall. I cannot bless you by asking for water, for you already stand over water. And I cannot bless you by asking that your fruit be delicious, for it is already delicious."

Then he said, "How shall I bless you? I shall bless you by asking that all new trees that come from your seeds shall be just like you."

When the angel ended the tale, God said, "You have told a wonderful story, and you have solved my problem, too. I will bless Abraham and Sarah in the same way. I will give them a child and a grandchild and many great-grandchildren. In time they will become a nation. And all of them shall say, 'May my children be upright and honest. May my children be wise. May my children love one another. May my children be just like Abraham and Sarah.'" [1,III:36]

From the Aggadah
JACOB AND ESAU—LIKE TWO PLANTS

Abraham and Sarah had a child just as God had promised. And they named the child Isaac. Isaac grew up and married Rebecca. And Isaac and Rebecca had twins, Jacob and Esau. Rabbi Levi used to say that, from the beginning, the twins were like two plants. The older one, Esau, was like a wild rose. And the younger one, Jacob, was like a myrtle tree. When their father, Isaac, saw them, he thought, "Esau shall be the next leader of the Jewish people."

But as the twins grew older, they changed. Esau began to worship idols, while Jacob spent his time studying the ways of God. Rabbi Levi said that they continued to be like the two plants. Like the wild rose, Esau grew thorns. And like the myrtle tree, Jacob's sweetness filled the tent with its perfume.

In his old age, Isaac's eyes grew weak, and he could not see the changes in his sons. But their mother, Rebecca, saw the changes and thought, "Jacob shall be the next leader of the Jewish people." [1,III:55]

THE BARGAIN

When Jacob and Esau were young, they made a bargain. Esau said, "I will take everything this world gives, and you can have everything God gives." Jacob agreed, and Esau thought, "I have outsmarted Jacob. I have taken everything that is really important. All he can hope for is a good place in heaven."

Many years later, Jacob returned from his journeys. He had two wives and many children. He had servants and cattle. He had silver and gold. Then Esau said to him, "You have cheated on our bargain. I was supposed to get everything in this world, and you were supposed to get only the things of heaven."

Jacob replied, "I have not cheated you. None of what I have belongs to me. Everything belongs to God. Yet God allows me to use these things as I need them." [1,III:86]

❧ 3 ❧

What Is a Promise Worth?

For many years, Joseph was in prison in Egypt. There time passed slowly, and Joseph spent his days remembering the past. Some of his memories made him happy: He remembered when his father gave him a beautiful coat. He remembered his mother's cooking. He remembered the dreams he dreamed, like promises straight from God.

Some of the memories made him sad: He remembered making his brothers jealous. He remembered telling them that he would one day rule over them. He remembered how they tore off his coat, threw him into a pit, and sold him into slavery. He wondered if things would have been different had he been a better son, a better brother, a better person.

Now he was in prison, though he had done nothing wrong. And he wondered if God had forgotten him, the way people forget a broken promise. He prayed and waited.

❧ ❧

One day the Egyptians came to his prison cell and said, "Pharaoh, king of Egypt, wants to see you."

Pharaoh sat in a huge room, on a platform on a throne, surrounded by priests, astrologers, and magicians—all dressed in fine robes. Joseph felt like the smallest man in the room. Pharaoh said, "They say you know the meaning of dreams. Explain my two dreams."

When Joseph heard the dreams, he knew that God had truly remembered him. Explaining dreams was a talent God had given him, just as some people are naturally good at sports and some people are naturally good at arithmetic.

Joseph told Pharaoh the meaning of his dreams, and Pharaoh believed every word. Then Pharaoh took a ring from his finger and gave it to Joseph, saying, "Next to me, you will be the most powerful man in all Egypt. Whatever you say, people will do. Whatever you command, people will obey. Without your word, no one in Egypt will lift his hand or raise his foot!"

Now the astrologers and the magicians were jealous. They asked Pharaoh, "Shall Egypt be ruled by a Hebrew slave who was bought in the marketplace for twenty pieces of silver? A ruler of Egypt must know the many languages of our peoples. Does this one know all our languages?"

Pharaoh said, "Tomorrow I shall test him to see if he knows our languages."

Joseph could not sleep that night. He prayed for help, and God sent an angel to teach him the languages of Egypt. Before dawn broke over the pyramids in the Valley of the Kings, Joseph was ready.

Pharaoh tested him. Each language Pharaoh spoke, Joseph answered in that language. Pharaoh was greatly pleased. "You have learned all the languages of Egypt," he said.

Then Joseph spoke to Pharaoh in Hebrew, but Pharaoh could not answer. "What language is this?" Pharaoh asked. "It is Hebrew," Joseph said, "the language of my people."

"Teach me this language," said Pharaoh. And Joseph and Pharaoh sat together day after day, but Pharaoh could not master Hebrew. Then Pharaoh said to Joseph, "Promise me—with your deepest promise—never to tell anyone that I could not learn your language." And Joseph said, "By my very life, I promise you I will never tell."

❦ ❦

Many years passed and many events occurred. Joseph's family came to Egypt. Joseph married and had children of his own. Then one day, Joseph's father, Jacob, called him. Jacob was ill and weak. He said, "I am dying. You must make me a promise, a deep, deep promise." Joseph replied, "Whatever you ask, Father." And Jacob said, "Promise me that after I die, you will take my body up to the Holy Land and bury me beside Abraham and Sarah." And Joseph promised.

Before Jacob died, Joseph went to Pharaoh and said, "I must leave for a while. I promised to take my father's body up to the Holy Land to bury him there." But Pharaoh replied, "Do not leave me. Go to your father and take back your promise."

Joseph thought for a long time. He thought about the promises God had made to him in dreams. He thought about the promise he had made to Pharaoh. He thought about the promise he had made to his father. Then he asked Pharaoh, "Can promises be made and broken so easily? If so, then let me take back the promise I made to you."

Now it was Pharaoh's turn to think for a long time. At last, he said to Joseph, "You are right. A promise is a promise. It should not be broken. So go to your Holy Land and bury your father there, just as you promised you would." [1,III:100]

From the Aggadah
PHARAOH'S TRICK

Rabbi Eleazar taught: When a Pharaoh died, another Pharaoh ruled, one after another. At first, the Children of Israel lived in peace in Egypt, but then came a Pharaoh who did not remember the good things Joseph had done for Egypt. Instead, the new Pharaoh looked at the Children of Israel and saw that they were growing into a mighty nation. He said, "They grow stronger each day. If war comes, they may turn against us. We must find a way to make them weaker." And so, like a fox hungry for sheep, Pharaoh plotted against Israel, saying, "We will make them slaves with hard labor."

Pharaoh decided to trick the Children of Israel to make them work harder. What did he do? He went to the Children of Israel and said, "I beg you to do a special favor for me. We need bricks for our

new city. Come and work beside me today." Then Pharaoh picked up a pail and shovel and went out to work. And every Israelite worked beside him all day long. Seeing the Pharaoh work hard made them work hard. By the end of the day, a great stack of bricks stood beside the river. But when darkness came, Pharaoh told his guards to count the number of bricks. When the bricks were all counted, Pharaoh said to the Israelites, "Now you are my slaves. Each day you shall make just this number of bricks!" [1,IV:8]

AN EGYPTIAN SAVED US

As a child, Moses was a prince in the palace of Pharaoh. But when Pharaoh learned that Moses was an Israelite, Moses had to flee for his life. So he ran into the wilderness. One day, he saw seven women come to a well to draw water. Suddenly, some shepherds came and tried to drive the women away. Moses stood up and helped the women. Then he gave water to their sheep. Later the women would say, "An Egyptian saved us," even though Moses was not an Egyptian. The rabbis told a story to explain this:

᷉ Once a lizard bit a man on the foot. Now the man ran down to the water to put his foot into it. But when he came to the water, he saw a child drowning. He reached into the water and saved the child. Then the child said, "Were it not for you, I would be dead." But the man said, "I was not the one who saved you. It was the lizard who bit my foot—he saved your life."

In the same way, when the women thanked Moses, he said, "I was not the one who saved you. It was Pharaoh, the Egyptian, who forced me to flee from Egypt—he saved your life." [1,IV:25]

❦ 4 ❦

Loving the Small Things

Our rabbis taught: During his many years in the wilderness, Moses was a shepherd, caring for the flocks that belonged to his father-in-law, Jethro. Then God tested Moses. It was a day like any other day. Moses rose early, taking the sheep to the foot of the mountain where the grass grew green and wild. He sat down to rest as the sheep began to graze. With quick little feet, one lamb scampered away from the flock. Moses followed the lamb, watching as it disappeared behind a rock. He hurried to the other side of the rock and saw that the lamb had found a little pool of water and was drinking from it. When Moses caught up with the lamb, he said, "I did not know you were thirsty, my little lamb. Now you must be tired from your running." So Moses put the lamb on his shoulders and carried it back to the flock. God thought, "This is the person I want to lead the Children of Israel out of Egypt. He takes such care of even the littlest lamb of another man's flock that I know he will take care of even the smallest baby among my flock, the Israelites."

❦ ❦

Someone asked Rabbi Joshua, "Why did God speak to Moses from a thorn bush?" Rabbi Joshua told this story: When it was time to tell Moses to go down to Egypt to set the Israelites free from slavery, God decided to speak from a tree. This caused all the trees to argue about which tree God should choose.

The fig tree said, "God should choose me. When Moses wandered through the wilderness, he went for days without water. He grew hungry, tired, hot, and thirsty. He did not know the way. But he saw the green leaves of my crown from a distance, and he knew that where I grow there is always water. He came to where I stood. How I welcomed him! He drank from the water at my roots. He ate my figs until his hunger was gone. He cooled himself in the shade beneath my branches. And when night came, he slept on the soft earth beside me. I have been Moses' friend, and that is why God should choose me."

But the carob tree disagreed, saying, "God should choose me. When Moses came out of the wilderness, he married Tzipporah, one of Jethro's daughters. She picked beans from my branches and ground the pods into flour. Then she baked the carob flour to make bread. At that holy moment of Moses' life, at his marriage feast, Moses blessed God over a loaf of carob bread. Moses used my fruit to give thanks to God, and that is why God should choose me."

Then each tree came and told why it was the most important tree to Moses. Some gave wood for the fires Moses used for warmth. Some gave shelter from the sun when Moses was out with the flocks. Every tree had a reason for being chosen. All but one, the lowly thorn bush, which did not speak at all.

God asked, "Thorn bush, why are you so quiet?"

The thorn bush said, "I am a small and unimportant tree. Animals hate me because they get caught in my branches. Human beings hate me because they prick themselves on my thorns. My branches are small and not very good for building fires or making houses. I am even too short for people to use for shade. There is no reason You should choose me."

But God said, "I have chosen you. I will speak to Moses from your branches."

Then all the trees asked, "Why should the Holy One choose this smallest and most hated of all trees?"

God replied, "To show that I am everywhere on the earth, even in the lowly thorn bush." [1,IV:26 and 30]

From the Aggadah
THE BURNING BUSH

On that day Moses turned aside to see the thorn bush, and it was full of wonders. Torah tells us that "the bush burned with fire, but the bush was not destroyed." God used the fire in the bush to teach

Moses a lesson. Moses was worried that the Egyptians would destroy the Children of Israel. But God said to Moses, "My people are like this thorn bush. The Egyptians burn them with hard work and try to destroy them, but My people cannot be destroyed."

Rabbi Joshua said: When God spoke from the burning bush, it was the first time that God spoke directly to Moses. God thought, "If I speak in the booming voice of thunder, I will terrify Moses. If I speak in a still small whisper, Moses will think he is talking to himself, and he will not pay close attention." So what did God do? The Holy One spoke to Moses using the voice of Moses' father. Moses answered, "Here I am, Father. What do you wish of me?" Then God said, "Moses, I am not your father. I am the God of your father, the God of all your ancestors. I used your father's voice because I know you love your father, and you are not afraid of your father. To save My people Israel, I need your love and not your fear." [1,IV:31 and 33]

MATZAH—THE SMALL MIRACLE

God said to Moses, "Go down to Egypt and tell the Pharaoh, 'Let My people go!'" But Moses was worried. "If Pharaoh lets the Children of Israel go, how shall I care for them? There are so many of them! Where will I find shade for them when the sun is hot in the wilderness? Where will I find houses in the wilderness to keep them warm in the winter? There are many women who are pregnant. There are many babies. What shall I do to protect the babies and the women too weak to march? There are so few trees in the wilderness and so little water, how will I find food and drink for all Israel?" God said, "Place your trust in Me, Moses. On the day the Israelites leave Egypt, I will teach them to make enough food for thirty days. Then you will see how I care for My people." So it was that the Israelites made the dough for their bread as usual, but on the day that Moses led them out of Egypt, there was no time for the dough to rise. The Israelites placed the dough on their backs, where it was baked flat by the sun. And this became the matzah that fed the Children of Israel for thirty days. In the same way, God provided all that the Children of Israel would need for the years they would spend wandering in the wilderness. [1,IV:35]

§ 5 §

A Time to Pray,
A Time to Act

After the ten plagues, Pharaoh let the Children of Israel go. The Israelites then were many in number. They were young and strong, old and weak. There were women who were pregnant, infants who had to be carried, blind people who had to be led, lame people who had to be helped. They could not march quickly. Even so, Moses led them out into the wilderness.

But Pharaoh's heart grew hard. He said, "Why have I let them go? Where will I find slaves to make my bricks and build my cities? I must get them back." So he summoned his soldiers. They were also many in number. They were young and strong, but they did not walk. Instead, they rode in chariots pulled by horses. And when Pharaoh gave the command, the chariots followed the Israelites, raising up great clouds of dust on the road where their wheels had passed.

Meanwhile, the Israelites came to the edge of the Sea of Reeds. They could not go forward because they stood before a great mass of water. Looking back toward Egypt, they saw a cloud of dust moving their way. And in the dust they saw the chariots of Pharaoh chasing

them. They were trapped, and even Moses was afraid.

One tribe said to another, "We must go forward." But no tribe wanted to be the first to step into the sea. Instead, the tribes argued. The tribe of Reuben said, "We will not go first. Send the tribe of Dan." The tribe of Dan said, "We will not go first. Send the tribe of Benjamin." And so it went—each tribe wanting another tribe to go first. And, all the while, the chariots of the Egyptians were coming closer and closer.

Nahshon, from the tribe of Judah, hated the arguing. His was the largest tribe, and he knew that something had to be done quickly. So he called out to all Israel, "Will you stand there and bicker while the chariots come? Perhaps Pharaoh has come to take us back to Egypt as slaves. Perhaps Pharaoh has come to murder us all. This is not the time to argue. Pick yourselves up and follow me!" Nahshon then sprang forward and ran into the sea.

Everyone watched to see what would happen. They crowded together, pushing forward. Children cried because they could not see, and some parents lifted their children onto their shoulders. And there was Nahshon, waist-deep in the water, his robe floating around him. He kept walking. Soon he was in the water up to his shoulders, and the Israelites could see only his head above the waves. Still he kept walking.

And what was Moses doing all this time? Moses stood on a hill beside the water, praying to God. He had started his prayers when the Israelites first reached the Sea of Reeds. But when he saw the chariots, he started to pray even louder. "God, O Holy God, help us! O Holy One, save us! Rescue us from the hands of the Egyptians as You promised You would."

As Nahshon walked into the sea, God spoke to Moses, saying, "My children are about to drown in the sea. The chariots of the

Egyptians are about to reach you. Why do you stand there praying?"

Moses asked, "O God, what else can I do?"

God replied, "Moses, there is a time to pray and a time to act. There is a time to pray to Me with many words and a time to be brief. Look, Nahshon has walked into the sea, and the water is up to his nostrils. This is the moment to save My people. Stop your praying and raise up your hands. Hold your rod up high where all can see it."

In the sea, Nahshon coughed. The water entered his nostrils and came up to his eyes, but he did not stop walking. Then Moses raised his rod, and God called out to the Sea of Reeds, "Make way for the Children of Israel. Stand aside. Let them pass through your middle on land that is dry." And the Sea of Reeds split in two, rising like two great blue walls on either side, leaving a dry dirt path through its very middle.

Even Nahshon was amazed. For a moment he stood alone on the path, coughing one last cough from the water he had swallowed. Then he heard the voice of Moses saying, "Go forward!" Nahshon turned to the people and cried out, "Follow me!" And the Children of Israel crossed the Sea of Reeds on dry land. [1,IV:82 and 83]

From the Aggadah
THE HORSES OF THE EGYPTIANS

Our rabbis taught: When the Children of Israel crossed through the Sea of Reeds, Pharaoh commanded his army to follow them. At first, the horses were afraid to move forward. They saw the towering walls of water on either side and refused to move. So God worked a miracle. All the waves of the sea shaped themselves to look like charging horses. Following the watery herd, the horses of Pharaoh's army charged into the sea. Now the soldiers riding in the chariots were afraid. They cried to their horses, "Yesterday we had to drag you to the Nile just to give you water to drink. Now you are dragging us into the midst of the sea." But the horses could not be stopped.

Pharaoh, however, could not go forward, for his horse still saw walls of water and refused to move. Pharaoh could only watch as his six hundred chariots rushed into the sea.

When the Egyptian chariots had gone halfway, the dry earth turned to mud. The wheels of the chariots were trapped. The horses grew exhausted trying to pull the wheels free. All at once, the walls toppled, and the sea rushed together, trapping the horses, the chariots, and the Egyptians.

Finally, Pharaoh's heart grew soft. At first, Pharaoh had thought he was mightier than God. When Moses had threatened to bring plagues on Egypt, Pharaoh did not believe that God could destroy him. Even after he let the Israelites go, Pharaoh still believed his army could defeat the God of Israel. But as he watched the sea swallow up his mighty army, Pharaoh at last understood the power of God. [1,IV:88]

GATHERING MANNA

Matzah had been the food of the Children of Israel, but when it was gone, there was no flour to make more. So God worked another miracle, sending manna to feed the people. And what was manna? The rabbis taught: Manna was bread, honey, and oil. When young people ate it, it made them strong as bread makes people strong. When old people ate it, it tasted as sweet as honey in their mouths. Because infants could not chew, manna turned to oil on their tongues. Every day the people went out and gathered enough manna to eat. On Friday, they gathered enough for two days so they would not have to work on the Sabbath.

The students of Rabbi Simeon asked, "Why didn't God just gave the Children of Israel enough manna for a whole year? In that way, they could gather it once and eat it all year long." Rabbi Simeon told this story: There was once a king who had a child. He decided to give his child an allowance. When the king gave enough money for a whole year, the child visited the king only once a year. So the king gave enough money for only a single day. In that way, the child came to visit every day. God gave us the manna every day to teach us that we must turn our hearts to God every day. [1,V:4 and 5]

⚕ 6 ⚕

God's Marvelous Voice

Before Moses led the Children of Israel to Mount Sinai, they were a ragtag collection of twelve tribes. When they left Sinai, however, they were one people. What happened to them at Sinai?

The Children of Israel heard the sound of the *shofar*. Moses said, "God is calling us to the foot of the mountain." So all the people came to the mountain.

Sinai was smoking. Every part of it was on fire. The flames were so bright that the people could not bear to look at them. The sound of the *shofar* grew louder and louder in their ears. The mountain sparked with lightning and shuddered with thunder. Moses spoke, and God answered from the flames. The people moved away from the mountain because they were afraid. But God said to Moses, "Tell the Children of Israel, 'You yourselves have seen that I talked with you from heaven.'"

Our rabbis taught: In that moment when the people heard the voice of God, every one of them—from the infant to the elder—understood God's words. You may ask, "How can that be? How could little children, who did not even know how to speak, under-

stand God's words? How did babies, who could not even understand their own parents, understand God's words?"

Rabbi Yose explained: It was like the manna they ate in the wilderness. To everyone who tasted the manna it tasted different. To some it was like bread, to some like honey, to some like oil. Just as the manna tasted the way each person needed it to taste, so were God's words heard by each person in the way that person needed to hear them.

Our rabbis taught: Even more, God's voice thundered throughout the world at that moment. How do we know this was true? At first, God's voice seemed to be coming from the south so the people moved to the south to hear it. But then the voice was coming from the north so they ran toward the north. Yet even as they ran, God's voice could be heard in the east. When they ran to the east to meet it, the voice sounded in the west. And when they ran to the west, they heard God's voice coming from heaven. They raised their eyes to heaven, and the voice of God came to them from the earth. The people were confused. "Where shall we find wisdom?" they asked. But wisdom was in the voice of God, and the voice of God was everywhere at once.

Our rabbis taught: God's voice was heard everywhere. The voice was like seven voices, and the seven voices became all the languages spoken by human beings. The thunder was very great, and the voice was so clear that it could be heard throughout the world. In speaking to the Children of Israel, God spoke to all the peoples of the world, speaking so every person in every land could hear the word of God. [1,V:40 and 41]

From the Aggadah
THE MENORAH

Moses stayed on Mount Sinai for forty days and forty nights. God spoke to Moses, and Moses studied God's words. "You must make a golden lamp with seven branches," God said, "and guard its flame so that it is always burning." Moses said, "O God, I am only a shepherd." But God answered, "Seek out the artist named Bezalel. He will create the *menorah*."

Still Moses was worried. "How will I tell Bezalel what You want," he asked. "No one has ever seen Your *menorah*."

"I will show it to you," God said, and fires rose around Moses on all four sides. In front of Moses the fire was white, behind him it was green, on his left it was black, and on his right it was red.

As God described the *menorah* for Moses, the flames twisted and twined, burning a drawing into the air. A column of twirling flame rose straight and tall as a tree. It sprouted feet of fire shaped like tree roots. Flames burst from the column. Six branches stretched out, three on each side.

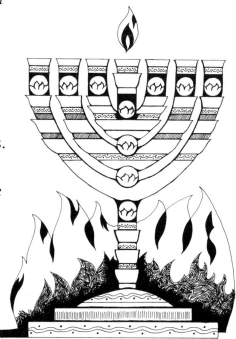

All at once, the branches blossomed, making flowerlike cups at their tops. The center column, too, formed a cup at its top. And in this center cup burned a single flame.

God said, "You may light any of the branches. But the center cup of oil shall always be burning. It is My *ner tamid*, My 'eternal light.' When you see it, you will remember that Your one God is always with you." [1,V:72]

THE TABLETS OF THE TEN COMMANDMENTS

God also commanded Moses to build the Ark of the Covenant, saying to him, "In this ark you shall place the stone tablets of the Ten Commandments." But what became of the two tablets of the Ten Commandments that Moses broke?

Rabbi Judah taught: There were two arks. When Moses first came down from Mount Sinai with the Ten Commandments, he saw that the people of Israel were worshiping a golden calf. Anger flared in him like a flame. He raised the two stone tablets and threw them to the ground, shattering them.

When God forgave the Children of Israel, Moses climbed the mountain again, returning with two new tablets of stone. Now these were the tablets of the Ten Commandments placed in the Ark of the Covenant. But Moses carefully gathered all the broken pieces of the first two tablets, placing them in another ark. In this way, Moses showed that everything God created is holy—not only those things that are whole, but even those things that to us seem shattered. [1,V:83]

❧ 7 ❧

Shall There Be One Law for Man and Another for Woman?

There came a time when Moses divided the land among all the tribes of Israel, giving each family a portion that would belong to that family forever. In this way, every man among the Children of Israel was given a portion.

But in the tribe of Manasseh, there were five women whose names were Mahlah, Noah, Hoglah, Milcah, and Tirzah. When their father Zelophehad died, none of them had yet married. And because there was no man in their family, they did not receive a portion of the Holy Land. Mahlah, the oldest, said to her sisters: "God created us equal to the men of Israel, but the men of Israel do not behave as if we were equal to them." Then Milcah said, "Moses taught us that God is good to all, and God's mercy is for all of Creation, not just for men, but for women, too." Hoglah said, "We must speak out." Noah said, "Let us go before the judges and ask for justice." And Tirzah said, "We deserve a portion of the land for our family although we have no man among us."

So the five sisters went to their local judge and said, "Give us a portion of the land as you have given it to other families. Although we have no man among us, we are equal to all other Israelites." The local judge, who was in charge of ten families, replied, "This is a hard case. I do not know how to judge it. Let us go to the judge who rules over me, the judge of fifty families." So the five sisters, with the judge of ten, went to stand before the judge of fifty families and said, "Give us our fair portion." But the judge of fifties said, "This case is too difficult for me. Let us take it to the judge of hundreds of families." So the five sisters, with the judge of tens and the judge of fifties, came to the judge of hundreds and asked him, "How will you decide?"

When the people of Israel heard about the five sisters, they came to the court of the judge of hundreds to see what he would decide. But the judge of hundreds was also puzzled. "Above me," he said, "is the judge of thousands. Let us take the case to him, for surely he will be wiser than I am." So the women and the judges and all the people came to the judge of thousands. And he said, "I, too, have a superior. Let us take this matter to the elders of all the tribes."

Standing before the elders, the judge of tens, the judge of fifties, the judge of hundreds, the judge of thousands, and all the people of Israel listened. The sisters said, "We have no man among us, but women are equal to men. Therefore, you must give us a portion of the Holy Land." The elders replied, "Let us take the case to Eleazar the Priest. He is wiser than we are." So they all went to Eleazar, but Eleazar said, "I cannot judge this case, for there is one even wiser than I. Let us take the case to Moses, our teacher."

So it happened that the judges, the elders, Eleazar the Priest, and all the people of Israel came to stand before Moses. The sisters spoke again, saying, "Our father died, and none of us is married. Yet we are members of the tribe of Manasseh. Our family should have a portion of the Holy Land equal to the portion of every other family." Moses

saw that the judges had asked the elders for wisdom, and the elders had asked Eleazar for wisdom, and Eleazar had asked him for wisdom. He thought, "If all these good people have asked for wisdom, I, too, should ask for wisdom."

"Wait here," Moses said to the five sisters, "for there is One who is even wiser than I. I shall take the case before God."

Then Moses went into the Tent of Meeting to pray. The people waited outside. Although there were many of them, they were silent. Some of them might have been praying, too—praying that God would give Moses wisdom.

After a while, Moses returned. "It is good that you came to me with this case," he said to the judges, the elders, and Eleazar the Priest. "It is good that all of us are together to hear this judgment," he said to all the people of Israel. "Pay close attention," Moses said. "God created us all equal. Male and female, God created us in God's own image. The daughters of Zelophehad deserve the portion of the land that belonged to their father. Equal justice: This is the law of Israel, and this is the law of God." [1,V:114 and 117]

From the Aggadah
AARON BRINGS PEACE

Our rabbis taught: Moses's brother, Aaron, was loved by all the people of Israel. So when Aaron died, the people wept for thirty days. "Aaron was a man of peace," they said. "He knew how to seek peace, and he knew how to love peace." When two friends had an argument, Aaron would go to one of them and say, "Look how your friend walks with his eyes down, wringing his hands in sorrow! Your friend truly misses you." Then Aaron would go to the other friend

and say, "Your friend is sorry for arguing with you. Look for your friend among the people!" The next time the two friends met, they would hug and kiss each other. In this way, Aaron brought peace to all the house of Israel. [1,V:109]

IN THE DAYS OF THE JUDGES

After Moses, Joshua led the Children of Israel. After Joshua, many judges came to lead the people. Our rabbis told this story: There was once a king with many subjects. He gave them food from his royal table so they would not starve. He built houses for them so they would have places to live. He planted vines for them so they would have grapes to make wine. He gave them flower gardens to bring them sweet smells. And he gave them trees for shade. But after the king's subjects ate and drank, they would trample the gardens, break the vines, and cut the trees for wood. And when the trees were gone, they would cut down the houses to make wood for their fires.

The king looked out from his palace and said, "What shall I do with my subjects? They behave like spoiled children!" So the king would punish them, and they would promise to behave better the next time. But when the next time came, they behaved again like spoiled children.

Our rabbis taught: This is what life was like in the time of the judges. The Children of Israel would forget God and bow down to the idols of the Ammonites. God allowed the Ammonites to punish them. Then God brought a judge to lead Israel, and the people promised never again to bow to idols. So God forgave them. But a short while later, the Children of Israel would forget God and bow down to the idols of the Philistines. And so it went, time after time. God said, "What shall I do with My children? All I wish is that they remember Me and follow the laws of My Torah!" [1,VI:16-18]

❧ 8 ❧

Deborah, Woman of Light

Day after day, Deborah studied Torah while her husband, Lappidoth, worked in the fields. At night, Lappidoth returned from his work to eat his dinner. Then Deborah said, "Listen to what I learned today," and she began to read to him the words of the Torah. But Lappidoth was tired from his work. His back ached, and his shoulders were sore. Whenever he heard Deborah say "Listen to what I learned today," he would prop his head in his hands and fall asleep.

Deborah said to herself, "God wants us to study Torah and do good deeds. I know that my husband is a good man, even if he does not study. I must help him to do good deeds." So she thought and thought until she came up with a plan. She twisted threads until they were thick as cords. Then she collected wax from the hives of bees and melted it, forming little towers around the threads.

One day, when Lappidoth came home from the fields, Deborah said, "Look, I have made candles. Take the candles to the holy place at Shiloh where the men sit and study the Torah day and night. In this way, scholars will study by your light, and you will have a

place among the wise." And Lappidoth did as Deborah asked.

God saw the wisdom of Deborah and said to her: "Because you have taken care to make the wicks thick so that the candles will give good light, I will call you 'woman of light.' Because you have cared for others and helped them, I will make your light shine for all Israel to see." Then God told Deborah to sit beneath a palm tree. "Many will come to you," God said. "You shall be a judge in Israel."

Far away, in the school of Elijah, a student heard this story and asked, "Can a woman be a judge?" Elijah taught: I call heaven and earth to witness that whether it be a Jew or a non-Jew, a man or a woman, a boy or a girl, the holy spirit will shine forth from any one of them who does good deeds. [1,VI:20]

From the Aggadah
RUTH AND NAOMI

In the days of the judges, a woman named Naomi lived in Moab with her two sons and their wives. When both of her sons died, Naomi said, "I will return to Israel, the land of my birth." Her daughters-in-law set out with her, but a short time later, one turned back. Then Naomi said to Ruth, her other daughter-in-law, "You, too, should go back to your people." But Ruth said, "Do not ask me to leave you. I wish to choose your religion as my religion. I want to convert and become a Jew like you."

When Naomi heard this, she said, "Let me tell you what it means to convert and become a Jew. From then on, you will not be able to go to the festivals where other people celebrate and worship idols." Ruth said, "Where you go I shall go." Naomi then said, "From now on, you must never live in a house that has no *mezuzah* on the door." Ruth responded, "Where you live I will live." But Naomi was not finished. "From now on," she said, "you must remember that your people are the Jewish people." Ruth answered, "Your people shall be my people." Finally Naomi said, "From now on, you must obey the laws of the one God." Ruth replied, "Your God shall be my God."

So it is written in the Book of Ruth, where Ruth says, "Do not ask me to leave you, to return from following after you. Where you go I shall go, where you live I will live. Your people shall be my people, and your God shall be my God." In this way, Ruth was converted.

And what was Ruth's reward? She married Boaz and had children. And her children had children. And, behold, one of her grandchildren was David, who would become king of Israel. [1, VI:47 and 51]

HANNAH'S PRAYER

Hannah was sad because she and her husband had no child. On one of the festivals, Hannah followed the crowds of Jews to Shiloh. She stood beside the holy place and prayed, "O God of hosts, look at all the people who gather to honor You. You have hosts upon hosts of people that You created in Your world. Is it too difficult for You to give me just one child?"

Rabbi Eleazar told this story to explain what Hannah had done: Once there was a king who gave a great feast for his servants. A poor man came and stood outside the door, begging, "Give me just a little piece of bread," but no one paid him any attention. So he forced his way into the hall and went up to the king. "Your Majesty," the poor man said, "you have made a great feast. Can you not find just a little piece of bread for me?" Then the king's heart was moved. He left his throne, found the best loaf of bread, and personally gave it to the poor man.

In the same way, Eleazar said, God's heart was moved by Hannah's prayer. God spoke directly to Hannah, saying, "Go home to your husband, Elkanah. In one year, you shall have a child. Call the child Samuel, which means 'God has heard,' for I have heard your prayer." And Samuel became a great prophet in Israel. [1,VI:54]

༄ 9 ༄

King David Studies Torah

King David held his harp on his knee. He strummed his harp and sang softly as he looked out the window. There was Jerusalem, his city, the City of David. He loved how the light of oil lamps showed through the windows of the homes, making the city sparkle. As he played the harp, he sang a poem of thanks to God, a psalm.

He smiled to himself. He loved being king. He was proud of his city. He was proud of his harp. He was proud of his psalm. And he was proud of his singing. Everyone said that his was the finest voice in all the land.

When he finished his song, he yawned and looked across the room. The couch he used for sleeping seemed to be calling to him. He felt tired, and it looked full of rest. He hung his harp on its hook by the window and took one last look. The moon was high over Jerusalem, a golden ball in a cloudless velvet sky. As he stretched out on the cushions of his couch, he closed his eyes and fell fast asleep, a smile still on his lips.

In the middle of the night, a breeze came up from the south, blowing into Jerusalem. It swirled into the open window of David's bedroom and made the harp swing back and forth on its hook. Like a million tickling fingers, the breeze crossed over and around the strings until the harp began to play sweet music. All the sounds of the night came to join it: the chirping of insects, the croaking of frogs, the mournful whooping of the hoopoe birds.

David sat up. Although he was wide awake, it seemed to him that he was still dreaming. What a beautiful song! he thought, as he listened to God's creatures sing. And still the breeze played on, moving the harp to and fro, a melody rising from the strings. David could not go back to sleep. He had to listen.

He lit the small oil lamp on the table and sat on his chair. He opened the scroll of the Torah that he kept on the table and began to study. In the place he opened the scroll the words read, "I will sing to God, for God has gained a glorious victory.... God is my strength, and God is my song!" So David studied and listened, listened and studied, until nearly the whole night had passed away. Then the breeze softened, and the harp came to a rest and played no more.

David prayed, saying, "O God, look how mighty I am! I am a great student of Your Torah, studying all night. And I am a great singer, singing to You all the time. Have You ever had any one who sings You more songs than I do?"

As soon as these words were out of his mouth, David heard a croaking noise that was louder than any noise he had ever heard before. David looked and saw a frog sitting on the window ledge. He thought, "Surely, I must be dreaming. How could a frog jump so high as to land on my window ledge?" And, even more magically, the frog began to speak.

"Is that a proper prayer for a king?" asked the frog. "You sound more like a rooster crowing. 'Look at me, how wonderful I am!' the rooster crows every morning. Those are good words for a show-off.

But are they good words for a king?"

David replied, "But it is all true. I am a good student of Torah. And I do sing songs to God all the time."

When the frog heard this, it jumped from the ledge of the window to the table. Sitting before the king. the frog said, "I like your songs, but I am tired of your bragging. I am an old frog, and you can learn a lesson from me. Long before God created human beings, frogs were already croaking, birds were already singing, and insects were already chirping. Every song we sing is a psalm for God. God created our songs for all the world to hear. You sing a little bit each night, and you brag that you are the greatest singer in all the world. But we frogs sing all night every night. We let our song speak for us."

David said, "Old frog, you are right. Sometimes when we are happy, we human beings brag too much about how great we are. It would be better if we were more like you. From now on, I will try to let the songs I sing and the things I do speak for me."

The frog said no more. It puffed up its throat and croaked a little song to God. David took his harp from its hook and began to play. And David and the frog sang together, sending their psalm to God, even as the sun rose up over Jerusalem. [1, VI:85 and 88]

From the Aggadah
DAVID AND THE SPIDER

Before David became king, he liked to sit on the roof of his house, enjoying the sunlight in the warm afternoons. Once, as he sat, he saw a spider spinning a web. As the spider moved from place to place, the sunshine caught the white wetness of the web and made it shine. David looked up into the heavens and said, "O God, what a strange creature you made! This spider has no real use. It wastes its time and all its efforts. It spins a web but makes no clothing. And in the end, all that is left is just a sticky mess."

But God answered, "Do not think that any one of My creatures is useless. The time may come when you may need even the spider."

Later, when King Saul had grown angry at David and was trying to kill him, David ran away and hid in a cave. But Saul was not far behind. He searched one cave after another, looking for David.

Now God called on a spider, and the spider spun a web that covered the opening of the cave in which David was hiding. When Saul reached that cave, he saw the web and said, "Surely, David could not have entered this cave, for he would have broken the web if he had tried to go in." So Saul passed by the cave.

When David awoke, he went to the opening of the cave and saw what the spider had done. "Spider, O spider," David said, "you have saved my life. Blessed is your Creator; blessed are you!" [1,VI:84]

WHEN WILL THE TEMPLE BE BUILT?

King David was loved by the people of Israel. Yet, even in Jerusalem, the City of David, there were a few who did not love him. What did these few do? At night, they would come to tease the king and try to make him angry. They would walk close by his windows and call out, "David, King David, when will the Temple be built? When will we be able to go into the house of God to worship?"

David heard their words, but he did not grow angry. He knew that God would not allow him to build the Temple, for David was a man of war, and God required that the Temple be built by a man of peace. In the end, David agreed with the men who came to tease him. "I, too, wonder when I shall be able to go to the house of God," he sighed. "I, too, long to see the Temple built."

One night, when the men came, David wrote a song for his Book of Psalms. He sang, "And I was glad when they said to me: 'If only we could go to the house of God.'" [1,VI:91]

§ 10 §

Solomon and the Snake

The snake was thirsty. It raised its head from the coil of its body and looked around. A man was coming its way, and the man was carrying a pitcher. At once, the snake made a plan. As the man came closer, the snake began to slither and moan. The man bent over and said, "Why are you moaning like that?"

"I am so thirsty," said the snake. "What do you have in your pitcher?"

"Milk," the man answered.

"Give me some milk," the snake said, "and I will show you where money is buried—enough money to make you rich."

So the man placed the pitcher of milk on the ground, and the snake drank from it. When the snake was finished drinking, the man said, "Now show me the money."

"Follow me," said the snake, slithering toward a large rock near the road. "The money is buried under this rock." And, sure enough, when the man moved the rock and dug into the soft earth, he found a bag of golden coins. He took the bag and leaning close to the ground, he began to tie it around his neck.

Suddenly, the snake leaped up and coiled itself around the man's neck.

"What are you doing?" the man asked.

"I am going to kill you because you were stealing all my money," the snake said, tightening its body around the man's neck.

"Stop," the man said. "You said you would trade me the money for the milk I gave you."

"No," said the snake. "I said only that I would show you the money."

"Stop!" said the man. "You have treated me unfairly, and you must come with me to the court of wise King Solomon. He will decide who is right."

So both came before Solomon. He was sitting in his court, holding his staff, and judging one case after another. Solomon saw that the snake was wound around the man's neck and that the man was trembling with fear. "Present your case," he said to the man.

Quickly, the man told his story: how the snake had been thirsty, how he had given the snake some milk, how the snake had promised money, and how the snake had tricked him.

"I will judge this case. But first," Solomon said to the snake, "you must get down off the man so that you and he are equal in my court."

Slowly the snake obeyed. It slithered off the man and coiled itself on the floor, sending its head high into the air. Then Solomon said, "Now, snake, you can speak. What do you seek?"

"Only what is written in the Torah," the snake answered. "God commanded snakes, 'You shall attack human beings.' I want to obey God by killing this man."

Then the king turned to the man, saying, "It is also written in the Torah that God commanded human beings to kill snakes." And with that said, Solomon handed his staff to the man, who struck the snake on the head and killed it. [1,VI:108]

From the Aggadah
BUILDING THE TEMPLE

Our sages taught: Iron was used to shorten the lives of human beings. As soon as people learned how to make things from iron, they began to make weapons of war from metal. God said, "Because the touch of iron is the touch of war, nothing in My Temple will be touched by iron." Just as war is the worst way to make peace, so, too, is building with iron the worst way to make a place of peace.

Rabbi Avin the Levite taught: The Temple held the tablets of the Ten Commandments and the Torah. From the Temple came the word of peace, the word of God, to make our lives longer and richer. When people build windows, they build them narrow on the outside and wide on the inside so that the light will come in and spread throughout the room. But when the windows of the Temple were built, they were narrow on the inside and wide on the outside so that the word of God could spread throughout the world. [1,VI:112 and 113]

GOD'S SPECIAL WORM

It was said that Solomon knew all the secrets of nature and spoke with the animals and the birds.

Once, as the curtain of evening drew across the sky, the eagle landed beside the king and said, "You seem troubled tonight, Solomon. What is bothering you?"

The king answered, "I am trying to solve a mystery: God commanded that I build a Temple to be God's house on earth. But God also commanded that no metal strike the stones of the Temple. How can we cut the stones from the hills without using iron axes? Still, there must be a way, for God would not command me to do the impossible."

The eagle replied, "God has created a way to cut stone without metal. But the secret is in the Garden of Eden."

"Then the secret is useless," Solomon answered sadly, "for God has commanded that no man or woman ever return to the Garden of Eden."

The eagle flapped its wings. "But God allows me to fly in and out of the Garden of Eden whenever I please. I will go now and bring you the secret when I return."

So the eagle flew away. Days passed. Then, at last, the eagle appeared with a nest in its talons. "Here is the secret," said the eagle, gently placing the nest on the ground at Solomon's feet.

Solomon looked into the nest. It was filled with tiny worms, each one the size of a grain of barley. As he watched, they wriggled and slithered. "What creature is this?" Solomon asked.

"This is the *shamir*," said the eagle. "The *shamir* eats rock. These little worms were created by God to help you make the Temple. They can cut the stones so that you do not have to use any metal."

"Thank you," said Solomon. "People say I am wise, but, truly, there is greater wisdom in God's creatures." [1,VI:111]

❧ 11 ❧

A Hundred Hidden Prophets

After the time of King Solomon, the kingdom was divided into two parts. The north was named Israel, and the south was named Judah. In time, Ahab became the king of Israel. Three times he went to war, and all three times he won. Then Ahab fell in love with Jezebel and married her. Jezebel brought idols and the priests of Ba'al to Israel. Jezebel ruled Ahab's heart. Jezebel and the priests of Ba'al ruled the people. Because the Israelites feared Jezebel, they worshiped Ba'al, while the name of the God of Israel was spoken only in whispers.

At that time, there were a hundred prophets of God in Israel. The prophets hated the idols, and they hated the priests of Ba'al. They knew that Ahab and Jezebel were sinning. But like the people, the prophets were afraid. Only Elijah was not afraid to speak God's words.

Like a wild man, Elijah would appear suddenly—now in this place and now in that place. Wherever he appeared, he spoke out against Ba'al, against Jezebel, and against Ahab. He spoke out against the idols and the priests of Ba'al. But before Ahab's men could find him, Elijah would disappear into the hills, living in caves, eating whatever he could find, wearing the skins of animals.

In Israel conditions went from bad to worse. Whatever Jezebel wanted, Ahab gave her. Because he loved Jezebel, Ahab built new temples for the priests of Ba'al and destroyed the altar of God.

Elijah could wait no longer. So he went to the prophets of God and said, "The time has come to destroy the idols and drive out the priests of Ba'al."

"We are afraid of them," the prophets said. "God does not stop them. Why should we?"

"What do you mean?" Elijah asked.

The leader of the prophets answered, "God has made Ahab the winner in three wars. God must love the king. Why else would Ahab win in battle?"

"It is not Ahab, but the Israelite soldiers who have won the wars," Elijah explained. "God loves the people of Israel because they are loyal to one another. Not once did a soldier turn against his friends. They stood together in battle, and none of them helped the enemy. For this reason, God gave them victory."

The leader of the prophets said, "If that is all God wants, then we shall also stand together—by hiding together. We shall hide until Ahab and Jezebel die, but not one of us will help Ahab."

"That is enough for ordinary people, but it is not enough for prophets," Elijah said. "If you will not go with me, I will go alone and defeat the priests of Ba'al. I will stand together with God."

Elijah called the priests of Ba'al to Mount Carmel for a contest between God and Ba'al. Four hundred priests of Ba'al stood on one side, and Elijah stood alone on the other side. All around, the people of Israel gathered to see the contest.

The chief priest of Ba'al mocked Elijah. "Are you alone, holy man? Where are all the prophets of your God?"

Elijah replied, "I, and only I, am left as a prophet of God."

The people heard Elijah's words, but they knew the truth: The hundred prophets of God were hiding. Yet not a single one of the Israelites told the king.

Because they stood together and did not help their enemy, God gave a great victory to Elijah and the Israelites that day. The priests of Ba'al were slain, and their idols were smashed to bits. And all the hundred prophets of God were saved. [1,VI:133]

From the Aggadah
LIKE THIS DAY ...

When the northern kingdom of Israel lost its war against Assyria, the people of Israel were led away in chains into slavery, never to be seen again. Afterwards, they would be called the "ten lost tribes," and many stories would be told about them.

According to one story, the sages, wanting to know if the ten lost tribes would one day return to the Land of Israel, searched the Bible for a verse that would foretell the future. In the last book of the Torah, the Book of Deuteronomy, the sages believed they found it. For there it is written, "God ... will cast them into another land, like this day."

Rabbi Akiva said: *Like this day* means that the ten lost tribes will never return, for this day happens only once. It never comes again.

But Rabbi Eliezer explained: *Like this day* shows that the sun comes up and goes down and returns again. In the same way, the sun went down on the ten lost tribes, and now they are in darkness. In the days to come, they will return with the light.

The sages remembered both teachings. Until this day, the story ends, our people wait to see which rabbi was right. [1,VI:149]

HEZEKIAH AND MANASSEH

Among the kings in Judah, Hezekiah was wise and good. But his son, Manasseh, was nothing like his father. When Hezekiah was king, he taught the Torah to all the people of Judah. He also taught them the wise sayings of Solomon from the Book of Proverbs. But Manasseh brought idols into Jerusalem and taught the people to bow down to the idols and worship them.

Our sages asked if Hezekiah had taught the Torah to everyone but had forgotten to teach it to his own son. And they answered their own question, "Of course not. The good Hezekiah spent hour after hour teaching his son the words of the Torah, but the son was stubborn and refused to listen to his father."

Manasseh said, "These are the words and the wisdom of the past. Why should I pay attention to them?"

To this day, we remember the teachings of King Hezekiah and the sins of King Manasseh. We rejoice when we hear the name Hezekiah, but we are sad when we hear the name Manasseh. [1,VI:172]

❦ 12 ❦

Jeremiah and Moses

When the armies of Babylon came to destroy Jerusalem and the Children of Israel, God said to the angels, "Babylon is mighty. Jerusalem will be lost to flames. Even My Temple will be left in ruins. But My people cannot be destroyed."

The angels said, "Can the Temple be destroyed? Can human beings ruin the place where God dwells?"

God answered, "I promised that I would always stand with the Children of Israel. Soon, Babylon will capture the people and take them from the land. I must go where the Children of Israel go. So I shall leave the Temple, and when I leave, the Babylonians will destroy it. When the people return to build a new Temple, I shall return with them."

The angels began to weep. "See how the city burns and the people suffer!"

God said, "The time for weeping is come. On this day, the Temple will be ruined."

Early in the morning, God's voice came to the prophet Jeremiah: "Go and teach the Children of Israel how to weep for the Temple.

Cry out to Moses. Let the greatest prophet of My people weep for the end of Jerusalem."

Jeremiah said, "O God, no one knows where you buried Moses."

God said, "Call out from the banks of the river Jordan. Moses will hear your cry."

Then Jeremiah went and cried out, "Moses, O Moses, you are needed on this day." And as Jeremiah cried, he heard the echo of his voice coming back from the hills on the other side of the river.

Then Jeremiah heard another voice like an echo, but this time it was the voice of Moses saying, "Why am I needed on this day, more than on any other?"

Jeremiah answered, "God has called you to come to Jerusalem."

So Moses went to the angels and found them weeping. He asked, "Why am I needed on this day, more than on any other?"

"Do you not know? On this day the Temple will be destroyed."

Then Moses grabbed the sleeve of his robe and ripped it. Tears filled his eyes. He called to the spirits of Abraham and Sarah; Isaac and Rebecca; Rachel, Leah, and Jacob. "Rise up and go with me to Jerusalem. On this day, the Temple is dying, and we must be there." And together they went, their heads bent in sorrow, weeping and mourning, to the gates of the Temple.

God saw that Jeremiah and Moses and all the great fathers and mothers of the Jewish people had gathered at the gate of the Temple. And God said to the angels, "Now I can leave the Temple and let it die. The Children of Israel will hear words of comfort from their leaders. And they will remember the Jewish past, so they can dream of a Jewish future." [1,VII:11]

From the Aggadah
THREE PROPHETS

Rabbi Eliezer ben Jacob taught: Three prophets went with the captured Children of Israel to Babylonia. In Babylonia, the first prophet taught the people to remember the Temple. He taught them the size of the altar, the names of the gates, even the height of the walls. Remember these things, he told them, so that when the time is right, you can build the Temple again.

The second prophet taught the people that they could continue their prayers, although the Temple was destroyed. "Sing God's praises," he said, "even in this foreign land. For we are God's people, and God is with us wherever we go." So the people built synagogues. And they sang God's song, even by the rivers of Babylon.

The third prophet taught the people that the Torah should be written in the square letters used in Babylon. "The children will be used to these letters," he said, "and they will love the Torah more if it is easy for them to read." And to this very day, we still read Hebrew in the square letters we learned in Babylonia. [1,VIII:8]

FOOLISH HAMAN

Haman came and tried to destroy the Jewish people in Persia. The people were saved by Mordecai and Esther. And it came to pass that Haman was destroyed.

Our sages told the following story:

℘ A bird made its nest at the edge of the sea, and the waves came and swept the nest away. What did the bird do? It took sand in its beak and threw the sand into the sea. Then it took water into its beak and threw the water on the sand. Over and over, it kept doing this.

Another bird came and said, "What are you doing?" And the first bird replied, "I will not leave this place until I turn the sea into dry land and the dry land into sea."

The other bird said, "You are the biggest fool in the world. With all your work, you cannot change sand to sea, or sea to sand."

Our sages taught: So it was with Haman. For Haman could no more destroy God's people than a bird could change the sea into dry land or the dry land into the sea. And so the Jews lived, and Haman died. [1,VIII:22]

About the Author

SEYMOUR ROSSEL is the publisher of the UAHC Press and the author of more than twenty books for Jewish and public schools, including the two-volume best-seller *A Child's Bible; Journey through Jewish History; The Holocaust; Israel: Covenant People, Covenant Land;* and *A Thousand and One Chickens.*

About the Illustrator

JUDY DICK, a graduate of Yeshiva University, attended the Fashion Institute of Technology and holds a degree in illustration from Pratt Institute. She is a free-lance illustrator, who has coordinated art and Jewish studies, while working on projects in the United States, Israel, and the former Soviet Union.